KU-876-425

DON'T THINK OF YOURSELF AS BEING THE GOAT, CHARLIE BROWN...IF YOU FORGET ABOUT IT, EVERYONE ELSE WILL, TOO..
DO YOU REALLY THINK SO, LUCY?
I'M POSITIVE!
GOOD NIGHT, GOAT!

# SLIDE, CHARLIE BROWN! SLIDE!

VOL. II from IT'S A DOG'S LIFE, CHARLIE BROWN!

---

## Charles M. Schulz

CORONET BOOKS
Hodder Fawcett Ltd., London

Copyright © 1960, 1961, 1962 by United
Feature Syndicate, Inc.
First published by Holt, Reinhart and
Winston, Inc.
First Fawcett Crest printing 1968
Coronet Edition 1969
Second Impression 1969
Third Impression 1970
Fourth Impression 1971
Fifth Impression 1973
Sixth Impression 1974
Seventh Impression 1975

---

This book is sold subject to the condition that it shall not, by way of trade or otherwise, be lent, re-sold, hired out or otherwise circulated without the publisher's prior consent in any form of binding or cover other than that in which this is published and without a similar condition including this condition being imposed on the subsequent purchaser.

Printed and bound in Great Britain for
Coronet Books,
Hodder Fawcett Ltd,
St. Paul's House, Warwick Lane,
London, EC4P 4AH
by Hazell Watson & Viney Ltd,
Aylesbury, Bucks

ISBN 340 0 04407 1

I JUST DON'T WANT TO SEE BEETHOVEN'S BIRTHDAY COMMERCIALIZED!
COMMERCIALIZED?
YES, COMMERCIALIZED!
THE NEXT THING YOU KNOW THEY'LL BE SELLING BEETHOVEN SWEAT-SHIRTS!
DID SOMEONE MENTION BEETHOVEN SWEAT-SHIRTS?

YOU THINK GIVING GIRLS PRESENTS WILL BE COMMERCIALIZING BEETHOVEN'S BIRTHDAY?
WELL, HOW LONG DO YOU THINK IT CAN BE KEPT FROM BEING COMMERCIALIZED? DON'T BE NAIVE!
DO YOU THINK IT CAN BE KEPT NON-COMMERCIAL FOREVER?! GOOD GRIEF! SOMETIMES YOUR NAIVETINESS AMAZES ME!
"NAIVETINESS"?

YOU? YOU ADMIT YOU WERE WRONG? YOU? YOU?!
OF COURSE, CHARLIE BROWN.. AND I'LL ADMIT THAT I'VE BEEN WRONG BEFORE...
I REMEMBER THE LAST TIME I WAS WRONG ABOUT SOMETHING.. IT WAS IN 1958, I THINK... ALONG IN JULY SOMETIME, OR WAS IT IN AUGUST? YES!
THE LAST TIME I WAS WRONG WAS IN AUGUST, 1958.. I THINK IT WAS ON A MONDAY, AND...
OH, GOOD GRIEF!

THIS WRITER SAYS THAT CHILDREN ARE REMARKABLY OBSERVANT..
HE SAYS THAT CHILDREN ARE MUCH MORE AWARE OF WHAT IS GOING ON AROUND THEM THAN ADULTS THINK THEY ARE
I'M RATHER INCLINED TO AGREE WITH HIM, AREN'T YOU?
HUH?

I WOULD NEVER THINK OF STEALING COOKIES FROM A STORE!
NO, NEITHER WOULD I!
BUT FROM HOME... THAT'S DIFFERENT..
OH, YES, IT'S PERFECTLY ALL RIGHT TO STEAL THEM FROM YOUR MOTHER AT HOME
THAT'S WHAT IS KNOWN AS A DOUBLE STANDARD OF MORALITY!

GOOD GRIEF! IT'S MORNING ALREADY!
THIS IS THE DAY OF OUR FIRST GAME
I'M NO MANAGER...I CAN'T RUN A BASEBALL TEAM...EVERYBODY KNOWS I'M A LOUSY MANAGER... NOBODY EVEN PAYS ANY ATTENTION TO ME...THEY ALL HATE ME...
I THINK I'LL JUST STAY IN BED... MAYBE IT'LL RAIN...MAYBE NO ONE ELSE WILL SHOW UP EITHER.. I'LL JUST STAY IN BED, AND...
OKAY, MANAGER! RISE, AND SHINE!

I CAN'T GO OUT THERE TODAY, LUCY.. I'M NO GOOD AS A MANAGER.. I'M SCARED!
SCARED? WHY, YOU BLOCKHEAD!
YOU WANTED TO BE THE MANAGER, AND YOU'RE GOING TO BE THE MANAGER! NOW, YOU GET OUT THERE AND MANAGE!!!
BOOT
HI, CHARLIE BROWN! WHERE HAVE YOU BEEN? WE'VE BEEN WAITING FOR YOU...
WELL, AT FIRST I THOUGHT I WOULDN'T BE ABLE TO MAKE IT, BUT I FINALLY GOT HERE UNDER THE INFLUENCE OF INFLUENCE!

ONE FINGER MEANS A FAST BALL AND TWO FINGERS MEAN A CURVE..
MMM
THREE FINGERS MEAN A DROP AND FOUR FINGERS MEAN A PITCH-OUT...
WHAT IF I FORGET?
DON'T WORRY ABOUT IT...WE ONLY HAVE SIGNALS TO FOOL THE OTHER TEAM INTO THINKING YOU CAN THROW SOMETHING BESIDES A STRAIGHT BALL.
IT'S ALWAYS NICE TO WORK WITH A CATCHER WHO HAS REAL CONFIDENCE IN YOU!

OKAY, HERE WE GO! THE FIRST PITCH OF THE FIRST GAME OF THE SEASON!
THIS YEAR I'M DETERMINED! THIS YEAR THINGS ARE GONNA BE DIFFERENT! THIS YEAR I'M REALLY GONNA THROW 'EM IN THERE!
I CAN'T STAND IT...

BONK!
YOU DIDN'T EVEN TRY TO CATCH IT! IT FELL RIGHT NEXT TO YOU!!
THEY SCORED FOUR RUNS!! WHAT'S THE MATTER WITH YOU?!
HOW CAN I PLAY BASEBALL WHEN I'M WORRIED ABOUT FOREIGN POLICY?

A HUNDRED AND TWENTY-THREE TO NOTHING!
GOOD GRIEF! WHAT A WAY TO LOSE YOUR FIRST GAME OF THE SEASON..
WHERE DID EVERYBODY GO?
THEY ALL WENT HOME TO CRY..
SNIF
ALL OF THEM?
ALL OF THEM!
SNIF!
WAAH

I DREAMED ABOUT YOU LAST NIGHT, SCHROEDER..
I DREAMED THAT YOU GAVE UP THIS STUPID PIANO, AND WENT TO TRADE SCHOOL TO LEARN HOW TO MAKE A LIVING SO YOU COULD SUPPORT ME AFTER WE GOT MARRIED!
THE ONLY WAY I WOULD EVER MARRY YOU WOULD BE IF YOU WERE THE LAST GIRL ON EARTH, AND IN THAT CASE ALL THE TRADE SCHOOLS WOULD PROBABLY BE GONE, TOO!
I'LL HAVE TO ADMIT THAT SOUNDS LOGICAL!

IT'S DISGRACEFUL THE WAY YOU HANG AROUND ALL DAY DOING NOTHING!! NOW YOU GET OUT THERE, AND CHASE SOME RABBITS!
ARF ARF ARF
YOU'RE NOT FOOLING ANYBODY BUT YOURSELF!

PUNT!
I HAD NO IDEA THAT PUNTING COULD BE SO SOUL-SATISFYING!

THAT'S ODD...
LAST NIGHT I LEFT MY FOOTBALL IN THE BACK YARD, AND THIS MORNING IT'S IN THE FRONT YARD...
VERY PECULIAR...
THE "MAD PUNTER" STRIKES AGAIN!
PUNT!

I DIDN'T TAKE YOUR STUPID OL' FOOTBALL!
WELL, SOMEBODY DID!
SOMEBODY'S BEEN KICKING IT ALL OVER THE NEIGHBORHOOD, AND I'D LIKE TO KNOW...
WUMP
THE "MAD PUNTER" HAS STRUCK AGAIN!

IT'S FANTASTIC!
ONE MINUTE MY FOOTBALL IS IN THE FRONT YARD, AND THE NEXT MINUTE SOMEBODY HAS PUNTED IT INTO THE BACK YARD
BUT **WHO**? THERE ISN'T A **HUMAN BEING** IN SIGHT!
HEE HEE HEE HEE HEE HEE

TV! TV! TV!
ALL YOU EVER DO LATELY IS SIT, AND WATCH TV!!
I BEG YOUR PARDON...I AM NOT WATCHING TV...
I AM ENGAGED IN CREATIVE VIEWING!!

DOES IT REALLY MAKE YOU HAPPY TO TEAR ME DOWN, LUCY?
DOES IT REALLY MAKE YOU HAPPY TO KNOW THAT ALL YOUR INSULTS ARE HURTING ME?
DO I LOOK HAPPY?
I COULDN'T DENY IT!

I CAN'T LOOK!
THE SCORE IS THREE TO TWO IN THE LAST OF THE NINTH!
BUT WE HAVE TWO OUTS!
BUT CHARLIE BROWN IS ON THIRD! AND OUR BEST HITTER IS COMING UP!
SAY, YOU DON'T THINK CHARLIE BROWN WILL TRY TO STEAL HOME, DO YOU?
NEVER! NOT EVEN CHARLIE BROWN WOULD DO ANYTHING THAT STUPID!
I WONDER IF I SHOULD TRY TO STEAL HOME !?

THIS IS MY BIG CHANCE TO BE A HERO!
IF I COULD STEAL HOME, THE GAME WOULD BE ALL TIED UP, AND I'D BE THE HERO!
I HAVEN'T GOT THE NERVE!

I'M GONNA STEAL HOME, AND I'M GONNA BE A HERO!
GET READY NOW....HERE I GO...DON'T BE A COWARD.... HERE I GO...DON'T BE SCARED...
HERE I GO....ZOOM....HERE I GO...DON'T BE A COWARD... HERE I GO...DON'T BE SCARED...
HERE I STAY!

I GOTTA TRY IT!
IF I'M GONNA BE A HERO, I GOTTA TRY TO STEAL HOME!
FIRST I'LL DANCE AROUND A LITTLE ON THE BASELINE TO CONFUSE THEIR PITCHER...
...AND THEN I'LL...
TAKE OFF!

CHARLIE BROWN IS TRYING TO STEAL HOME!!
SLIDE, CHARLIE BROWN! SLIDE!
OH, YOU BLOCKHEAD!

WHAAAH! WE LOST THE GAME ALL BECAUSE OF CHARLIE BROWN WHHAAAAAHHH!!
WAS I OUT?
OUT?! WHY, YOU BLOCKHEAD, YOU DIDN'T EVEN GET HALF WAY HOME!
RATS!

WHY DID I HAVE TO GO AND TRY TO STEAL HOME?
WHY? WHY? WHY?
I THOUGHT I HEARD A CRY OF ANGUISH..
WHY? WHY? WHY? WHY? WHY?
WHY? WHY? WHY? WHY?

WHY DIDN'T I JUST WAIT ON THIRD BASE? WHY DID I HAVE TO TRY TO STEAL HOME?!
WHY? WHY? WHY? WHY?
CHARLIE BROWN?
I HAVE BEEN ASKED TO TELL YOU THAT YOUR CRIES OF ANGUISH ARE KEEPING THE WHOLE NEIGHBORHOOD AWAKE!
WHY? WHY? WHY? WHY?

IF I HAD STOLEN HOME, I'D HAVE BEEN THE HERO...INSTEAD I'M THE GOAT
DON'T THINK OF YOURSELF AS BEING THE GOAT, CHARLIE BROWN...IF YOU FORGET ABOUT IT, EVERYONE ELSE WILL, TOO..
DO YOU REALLY THINK SO, LUCY?
I'M POSITIVE!
GOOD NIGHT, GOAT!

ALL I WANTED TO DO WAS BE A HERO...
BUT DO I EVER GET TO BE A HERO? NO! ALL I EVER GET TO BE IS THE STUPID GOAT!
DON'T BE DISCOURAGED, CHARLIE BROWN... IN THIS LIFE WE LIVE, THERE ARE ALWAYS SOME BITTER PILLS TO BE SWALLOWED..
IF IT'S ALL THE SAME WITH YOU, I'D RATHER NOT RENEW MY PRESCRIPTION!

DEAR TEAMMATES,
I HAVE BEEN THINKING OF RESIGNING MY JOB AS YOUR MANAGER, AND I
WE ACCEPT!
WAIT 'TIL I FINISH THE LETTER

CHARLIE BROWN, LET ME GIVE YOU A LITTLE ADVICE...
AS LONG AS YOU THINK ONLY OF YOURSELF, YOU'LL NEVER FIND HAPPINESS... YOU'VE GOT TO START THINKING ABOUT OTHERS!
OTHERS? WHAT OTHERS? WHO IN THE WORLD AM I SUPPOSED TO THINK ABOUT?
BEETHOVEN!
OH, GOOD GRIEF!

WHEN I GET BIG, I'M GOING TO BE A DOCTOR!
NO, I'M GOING TO BE MORE THAN A DOCTOR...I'M GOING TO BE A GREAT DOCTOR!
I WANT TO RISE TO THE GREATEST HEIGHT OF ALL...
I WANT TO WRITE A SYNDICATED MEDICAL COLUMN!

..AND YOU'RE WEAK, AND SPINELESS AND WISHY-WASHY!
SHE REALLY TOOK YOU APART, DIDN'T SHE, CHARLIE BROWN?
UH HUH...STEP BY STEP, VERSE BY VERSE AND LINE BY LINE...
YOU SOUND LIKE A VICTIM OF HIGHER CRITICISM!

LOOK! A LIBRARY CARD! I'VE TAKEN OUT A LIBRARY CARD!
I HAVE BEEN GIVEN MY CITIZENSHIP IN THE LAND OF KNOWLEDGE!
HOW POMPOUS CAN YOU GET?

WHAT IN THE WORLD IS SO GREAT ABOUT HAVING A LIBRARY CARD?
IT'S WHAT IT STANDS FOR! THEY TRUST ME! THEY'RE HONORING MY DESIRE FOR KNOWLEDGE WITH THEIR TRUST!
IN RETURN I'M SHOWING MY FAITH IN THEIR LIBRARY BY READING THEIR BOOKS... IT'S A COMMON BOND OF TRUST...
YOU HAVEN'T GOT A LIBRARY CARD... YOU'VE GOT A **TREATY**!

JUST THINK, CHARLIE BROWN... MY OWN LIBRARY CARD!
I HOPE YOU MAKE GOOD USE OF IT BY TAKING OUT ALL THE BOOKS YOU CAN READ..
I SUPPOSE THAT WOULD BE MORE PRACTICAL, WOULDN'T IT?
MORE PRACTICAL THAN WHAT?
I WAS THINKING OF HAVING IT FRAMED!

WELL, NOW THAT YOU HAVE YOUR LIBRARY CARD, AREN'T YOU GOING TO USE IT?
I CAN'T! I'M AFRAID TO GO INTO THE LIBRARY...
I JUST CAN'T MAKE MYSELF GO THROUGH THOSE DOORS...
I'VE GOT **LIBRARY FEVER!**
OH, GOOD GRIEF!

LOOK, LINUS... IT'S SILLY FOR YOU TO BE SCARED OF LIBRARIES..
BUT THEY'RE ALWAYS SO STILL.. AND WHEN YOU WALK IN, YOUR FOOTSTEPS ECHO LIKE YOU WERE IN A GREAT TOMB!
..AND THEN WHEN YOU GO UP TO THE FRONT DESK, THE LIBRARIAN LOOKS AT YOU WITH HER GREAT BIG EYES, AND SHE...
AAUGHH!

THERE'S ONE SURE WAY TO CURE SOMEONE OF BEING AFRAID OF LIBRARIES. HERE...GIVE ME YOUR LIBRARY CARD..
WHAT YOU NEED IS A LITTLE INSPIRATION...
WAP
WAP
NOW, HOLDING YOUR LIBRARY CARD HIGH, YOU MARCH PROUDLY INTO THE LIBRARY!
DON'T YOU FEEL INSPIRED?
I FEEL NOT UNLIKE A FOOL!
PUBLIC LIBRARY

I THINK I CAN UNDERSTAND YOUR FEAR OF LIBRARIES, LINUS...
"LIBRARY FEVER" IS SIMILAR TO OTHER MENTAL DISTURBANCES... YOU FEAR THE LIBRARY ROOMS BECAUSE THEY ARE STRANGE TO YOU...YOU ARE OUT OF PLACE...
ALL OF US HAVE CERTAIN AREAS IN WHICH WE FEEL OUT OF PLACE
OH? IN WHAT AREA DO YOU FEEL OUT OF PLACE, CHARLIE BROWN?
EARTH!

YOU'RE BEING **RIDICULOUS!**
NOW, YOU TAKE THAT LIBRARY CARD, AND YOU WALK UP THE STAIRS OF THAT LIBRARY, AND YOU GO THROUGH THOSE DOORS AND YOU TAKE OUT A BOOK!!
WHAT IF SOMEBODY SLUGS ME?

I DID IT! I WALKED RIGHT INTO THE LIBRARY, AND I TOOK OUT A BOOK!
THERE WAS NOTHING TO IT! IN FACT, ON THE WHOLE, IT WAS A RATHER PLEASANT EXPERIENCE
YES, SIR, A RATHER PLEASANT AND ENJOYABLE EXPERIENCE...
I'M STILL QUITE YOUNG, YOU KNOW... I MAY EVEN TAKE OUT ANOTHER BOOK SOMETIME!

THIS IS THE HEALTHIEST TIME OF THE YEAR..
YOU KNOW WHY? BECAUSE THERE'S MORE CALCIUM IN THE AIR THIS TIME OF THE YEAR, THAT'S WHY!
YOU SHOULD KNOW THINGS LIKE THAT, LINUS...
WELL-INFORMED LAYMEN MAKE UP THE FOUNDATION OF A HEALTHY SOCIETY!

I'LL SOCK YOU, CHARLIE BROWN!
I'LL WALLOP YOU, CHARLIE BROWN!
NOW, WAIT A MINUTE! HAS IT EVER OCCURRED TO YOU THAT THE REASON NATIONS CAN'T GET ALONG IS BECAUSE PEOPLE CAN'T GET ALONG? NOW, IF..IF TWO...
WHOP!
MY ONLY HOPE WAS THAT SHE'D TURN OUT TO BE A STUDENT OF POLITICAL SCIENCE!

SCHROEDER, I THINK IT'S DISGRACEFUL THE WAY LUCY BOTHERS YOU!
AND SHE'S ALWAYS ASKING EVERYONE, "WHY DOES HE HAVE TO PLAY THAT STUPID PIANO?" I THINK THAT'S TERRIBLE!
INCIDENTALLY, WHY DO YOU ALWAYS HAVE TO PLAY THIS STUPID PIANO?

YOU KNOW WHAT I SEE WHEN I LOOK AT YOU, CHARLIE BROWN?
I SEE **FAILURE**! I SEE FAILURE WRITTEN ALL OVER YOUR FACE!
JUST **LOOK** AT MY FACE...DON'T **WRITE** ON IT!
?

VIOLET SAYS I HAVE A "FAILURE FACE"...
OH, YOU **HAVE**, CHARLIE BROWN! YOU REALLY HAVE! IT'S GOT FAILURE WRITTEN ALL OVER IT!
I'VE NEVER SEEN ANYONE WHO HAD MORE OF A FAILURE FACE...
A REAL **FAT** FAILURE FACE!
I CAN'T STAND IT!

NOW, REMEMBER.. WHAT YOU ARE ABOUT TO SEE IS AN AUTHENTIC "FAILURE FACE"!
THEY'RE VERY RARE, AND YOU SHOULD LEARN TO RECOGNIZE ONE WHEN YOU SEE IT...
NOTICE HOW "FAILURE" IS WRITTEN ALL OVER IT? NOTICE HOW THE YEARS HAVE ETCHED "FAILURE" INTO EVERY LINE? NOTICE HOW...
GET OUT OF HERE!!

WHAT'S WRONG WITH YOU, CHARLIE BROWN?
WHY WON'T YOU LET MY BROTHER STUDY YOUR "FAILURE FACE"?
THINK OF HOW HE'LL BE ABLE TO STAND UP IN SCHOOL THIS FALL DURING "SHOW AND TELL" AND SAY HOW HE SAW AN AUTHENTIC "FAILURE FACE"!

CHARLIE BROWN, WHY ARE YOU STANDING WITH YOUR HEAD AGAINST THAT TREE?

Z
DID YOU HEAR ABOUT THE NEW FREEWAY?
SNOOPY
IF THEY BUILD IT ACCORDING TO PLAN, IT'LL RUN RIGHT THROUGH SNOOPY'S DOGHOUSE!
THAT DOESN'T SURPRISE ME A BIT...
SNOOPY
IT'S JUST ONE MORE INSTANCE OF MAN'S INHUMANITY TO DOG!

I CAN SEE IT ALL NOW! "MAKE WAY FOR THE FREEWAY!"
ENGINEERS RUNNING AROUND; TRUCKS RUMBLING BACK AND FORTH; BULLDOZERS PLOWING UP EVERYTHING...
..AND SUDDENLY IT'S GONE!
THE OLD HOMESTEAD!

WE CAN'T LET THEM BUILD A FREEWAY HERE, AND DESTROY SNOOPY'S HOUSE!
SNOOPY
MAYBE WE SHOULD WRITE A LETTER OF PROTEST...
TO WHOM?
I DON'T KNOW....HOW ABOUT SAM SNEAD? I'VE ALWAYS KIND OF ADMIRED HIM!

HAS THIS WORLD GONE MAD?!
SINCE WHEN IS A FREEWAY REALLY MORE IMPORTANT THAN A DOG'S HOME? HAVE WE LOST OUR SANITY?
HAVE WE LOST OUR PERSPECTIVE? DOESN'T THE LOVE AND THE LOYALTY OF A DOG MEAN ANYTHING TO US ANYMORE?
THAT'S GREAT ORATORY, CHARLIE BROWN!
CLAP CLAP CLAP

ALL RIGHT, SO THEY RUN A FREEWAY THROUGH HERE, AND YOU LOSE YOUR DOGHOUSE...
SNIF!
YOU THINK YOU'RE THE FIRST ONE WHO'S EVER LOST HIS HOME? YOU THINK YOU'RE THE ONLY ONE? HUH?!
STOP FEELING SO SORRY FOR YOURSELF!
WHATEVER HAPPENED TO GOOD OL' FASHIONED "ARM-AROUND-THE-SHOULDER" SYMPATHY?

I'VE MADE UP MY MIND! IF THEY'RE GOING TO PLOW UP MY HOUSE FOR A FREEWAY, THEY'RE GOING TO HAVE TO PLOW ME UP WITH IT!
YOU'RE FACING THE WRONG WAY...IF THE BULLDOZERS COME, THEY'LL COME FROM THAT DIRECTION..
I'VE MADE UP MY MIND! IF THEY'RE GOING TO PLOW UP MY HOUSE FOR A FREEWAY, THEY'RE GOING TO HAVE TO PLOW ME UP WITH IT!

HERE COME THE BULLDOZERS!
AAGH!
NO, YOU'RE GOING TO HAVE TO DO BETTER THAN THAT

READY? LET'S TRY IT AGAIN...
HERE COME THE BULLDOZERS!
WOOF!

YOU'VE GOT TO STAND FIRM, SNOOPY!
YOU'VE GOT TO SHOW 'EM THEY CAN'T BUDGE YOU...NOW, LET'S TRY IT AGAIN...
HERE COME THE BULLDOZERS!
WOW! THIRTY FEET!

ALL RIGHT, LET'S PRETEND THEY'VE STARTED TO BUILD THE FREEWAY...
THE BULLDOZERS COME UP, AND THEY SEE YOU HAVE REFUSED TO VACATE...SO THEY CALL OVER THE FOREMAN...
THE FOREMAN COMES UP TO YOU, AND SAYS, "WHAT'S THE BIG IDEA?" NOW, WHAT DO YOU DO?
NO, I'M AFRAID FAINTING WON'T HELP A BIT!

I JUST KNOW THAT THIS IS THE END!
THOSE BULLDOZERS WILL BE HERE THE FIRST THING ON MONDAY MORNING TO WIPE ME OUT!
SNOOPY
THE NIGHT IS DARK AND I AM LONELY... THERE ARE SO MANY THINGS I'VE LEFT UNSAID... SO MANY THINGS LEFT UNDONE...
RATS!

YOU'VE BEEN REPRIEVED, SNOOPY!
THIS IS NATIONAL DOG WEEK! THEY'D NEVER DARE TO TEAR DOWN YOUR HOUSE TO BUILD A FREEWAY DURING NATIONAL DOG WEEK!
YOU HAVE A SEVEN DAY REPRIEVE!
THANK YOU, MADISON AVENUE!

GOOD GRIEF, THIS IS FRIDAY ALREADY!
SNOOPY
THAT MEANS MY REPRIEVE IS ALMOST UP, AND I HAVE TO START WORRYING ABOUT THAT FREEWAY BUSINESS AGAIN...
I CAN'T STAND IT! I JUST CAN'T STAND IT!
WHY HAVE I NO FRIENDS IN HIGH PLACES?!!

ONE MORE DAY AND THE BULLDOZERS COME..
ON MONDAY MORNING THEY'RE GOING TO DESTROY MY HOUSE JUST TO BUILD A FREEWAY...
SIGH
YOU'VE BEEN A GOOD HOME!

I DON'T MIND PLAYING RIGHT FIELD
I DON'T MIND STANDING OUT HERE IN WEEDS OVER MY HEAD...REALLY, I DON'T...
I MEAN, IF THIS IS WHERE I CAN DO THE TEAM THE MOST GOOD, THIS IS WHERE I BELONG
THE ONLY THING THAT BOTHERS ME IS I DON'T KNOW IF I'M **FACING** THE RIGHT WAY!

WE WANT TO JUMP ROPE, SNOOPY...
IN FACT, WE WANT TO JUMP ROPE RIGHT WHERE YOU'RE SITTING....SO **MOVE**!
IF THIS HAD BEEN NATIONAL DOG WEEK, I NEVER WOULD HAVE MOVED!

LOOK, LUCY, THIS IS OUR LAST GAME OF THE SEASON..
CAN'T YOU PLAY ANY BETTER THAN YOU'VE BEEN PLAYING?
YOU'VE DROPPED FIVE FLY BALLS THIS INNING!
YOUR CAP IS TOUCHING MY CAP, CHARLIE BROWN...
MOVE YOUR HEAD SO YOUR CAP WON'T TOUCH MY CAP...
WHENEVER A MANAGER TALKS TO ONE OF HIS PLAYERS, HE SHOULD MAKE SURE THAT HIS CAP DOESN'T TOUCH THE PLAYER'S CAP...
I CAN'T STAND IT!

SO THIS IS THE PITCHER'S MOUND, EH?
BOY, YOU CAN SEE A LONG WAY FROM UP HERE...I'LL BET YOU CAN SEE FOR TEN MILES...
IT WOULD BE NICE TO COME UP HERE IN THE EVENING, AND JUST LOOK AROUND...MAYBE EVEN BRING A FEW FRIENDS...
I'LL HAVE TO THINK ABOUT THAT!

IF YOU CAN GET THIS LAST MAN OUT, CHARLIE BROWN, WE'LL WIN THE BALL GAME...
..THEREFORE, I WOULD SUGGEST YOU THROW HIM A CURVE!
NO, DON'T DO THAT! THROW HIM A DROP!
HOW ABOUT A KNUCKLE-BALL?
OR A SLIDER?
HOW ABOUT A SLOW BALL?
GIVE 'IM THE OL' HIGH, HARD ONE!
CAN YOU THROW AN UPSHOOT?
THIS WORLD IS FILLED WITH PEOPLE WHO ARE ANXIOUS TO FUNCTION IN AN ADVISORY CAPACITY!

YOU'D BETTER PITCH THIS NEXT GUY SOMETHING PRETTY TRICKY, CHARLIE BROWN..
I'D LIKE TO SEE YOU THROW HIM AN "EXPECTORATE BALL," BUT I GUESS YOU CAN'T
THEY'VE BANNED THE "EXPECTORATE BALL" SO THERE'S NO SENSE IN EVEN TALKING ABOUT IT!
IF YOU STAND ON A PITCHER'S MOUND LONG ENOUGH, YOU MEET A LOT OF STRANGE PEOPLE!

I DON'T CARE WHAT ANY OF YOU SAY! I'M GONNA PITCH WHAT I WANNA PITCH!
THAT'S THE SPIRIT, CHARLIE BROWN! YOU PITCH JUST WHAT YOU WANT TO PITCH! DON'T LISTEN TO ANYONE ELSE! YOU PITCH JUST WHAT YOU WANT TO PITCH!
GOOD BYE, BALLGAME!

THIS GUY WILL NEVER BE EXPECTING A FAST BALL..
WITH THE BASES LOADED HE'LL BE EXPECTING A CURVE, BUT HE ALSO KNOWS I KNOW WHAT HE'S EXPECTING...
SO IF HE'S EXPECTING ME TO PITCH WHAT I KNOW HE KNOWS I KNOW HE KNOWS HE'S EXPECTING, I'D...
WHERE WAS I?

EITHER THIS GUY GETS A HIT, AND THEY WIN, OR I STRIKE HIM OUT, AND WE WIN...
EITHER HE'S A HERO, OR I'M A HERO! THIS IS IT! IT'S HIM OR ME!!
*SIGH* IT'S HIM...

A HOME RUN! GOOD GRIEF!
THUS ENDETH THE BALL GAME
AYE, THUS ENDETH THE BALL GAME!

SO YOU COULDN'T DO IT, EH, CHARLIE BROWN? YOU COULDN'T GET JUST ONE MORE MAN OUT!
YOU HAD TO LET HIM HIT A HOME RUN, AND WIN THE GAME! BOY, WHAT A PITCHER! WHAT A LOUSY PITCHER!!
I'M STILL AMAZED AT HOW FAR YOU CAN SEE STANDING HERE ON THE PITCHER'S MOUND..

WELL, THAT'S THE END OF ANOTHER MISERABLE SEASON! TWENTY GAMES LOST AND NO GAMES WON!
DIDN'T WE WIN ONE GAME BY FORFEIT?
NO, THE OTHER TEAM FINALLY SHOWED UP, REMEMBER?
OH, YES... I REMEMBER... WHAT A DIRTY TRICK!

I'VE WORKED UP SOME INTERESTING STATISTICS HERE ABOUT OUR BASEBALL TEAM, CHARLIE BROWN...
I THINK YOU'LL FIND THAT THEY SAY SOMETHING TO US...
LAST YEAR OUR OPPONENTS SCORED THREE THOUSAND AND FORTY RUNS TO OUR SIX! THEY MADE FORTY-NINE HUNDRED HITS TO OUR ELEVEN AND THEY MADE NINETEEN ERRORS TO OUR THREE HUNDRED...
TELL YOUR STATISTICS TO SHUT UP!!

I'M GLAD THE BASEBALL SEASON IS OVER FOR US!
I DON'T EVEN WANT TO HEAR THE WORD "BASEBALL" ANY MORE! I THINK IF I HEAR THE WORD "BASEBALL" AGAIN, I'LL SCREAM!
BASEBALL
AAUGH!

Z

I NEVER REALIZED THE WORLD WAS IN SUCH SAD SHAPE!
LOOK AT THIS NEWSPAPER... LOOK AT WHAT'S HAPPENING! I NEVER REALIZED THAT SUCH THINGS WENT ON TODAY!
WHAT ARE YOU READING, THE FRONT PAGE?
NO, THE MOVIE ADS!

GOING TO DO A LITTLE READING, EH, CHARLIE BROWN?
UH HUH...I ALWAYS TAKE OUT A BOOK DURING "NATIONAL LIBRARY WEEK"
IT DOES SOMETHING FOR THEIR MORALE...
LIBRARIANS LIKE TO FEEL NEEDED!

I DID JUST WHAT YOU DID, CHARLIE BROWN..
I TOOK OUT A BOOK FROM THE LIBRARY! THE LIBRARIAN WAS SO EXCITED!
SHE KEPT SHUFFLING THROUGH ALL THOSE CARDS ON HER DESK, AND THEN SHE'D MOVE HER INK PAD BACK AND FORTH AND SHE STAMPED EVERYTHING IN SIGHT!
I FEEL THAT FOR AT LEAST ONE LIBRARIAN I HAVE MADE "NATIONAL LIBRARY WEEK" A COMPLETE SUCCESS!

SOMETIMES I GET LONESOME FOR HOME...
BUT I SUPPOSE THIS IS BOUND TO HAPPEN WHEN YOU ARE AWAY FROM HOME...
I THINK THERE IS A NATURAL LONGING THAT WE ALL HAVE TO RETURN TO THAT PLACE WHERE WE WERE BORN OR RAISED!
HOW LONG HAVE YOU BEEN AWAY FROM HOME, CHARLIE BROWN?
FIFTEEN MINUTES!

Z
SNIF?
I KNEW I SMELLED A PICNIC GOING BY!

WELL, I'VE DISCOVERED A NEW TRUTH..
THERE ARE TWO CLASSES OF PEOPLE IN THIS WORLD WHICH ARE VIOLENTLY OPPOSED TO THUMB-SUCKING...
ONE OF THEM IS DENTISTS AND ONE OF THEM IS GRANDMOTHERS...
INTERFERING GRANDMOTHERS!!

WHAT IN THE WORLD ARE YOU DOING?
MY GRAMMA IS GIVING ME TROUBLE AGAIN...SHE KEEPS HIDING MY BLANKET!
SO?
SO I'M LAYING OUT DECOYS!

MY GRAMMA KEEPS TRYING TO HIDE MY BLANKET...
I HAVE TO BE PRETTY SHARP TO OUTWIT HER..
ISN'T THIS YOUR GRAMMA COMING NOW?

LINUS, WHY DON'T YOU PUT AWAY THAT BLANKET WHILE GRAMMA'S HERE?
YOU COULD JUST PRETEND TO GIVE IT UP, AND SHE'D NEVER KNOW THE DIFFERENCE....
BECAUSE I DON'T FEEL IT WOULD BE GOOD FOR HER TO HAVE HER OWN WAY....
HOW DO YOU EXPECT HER EVER TO BECOME **MATURE**?

GOOD NIGHT, GRAMMA!
I SUPPOSE I REALLY SHOULDN'T TEASE HER LIKE THAT...

SO YOUR GRAMMA'S GONE BACK HOME HUH, LINUS?
YUP...NO MORE FIGHTS OVER MY BLANKET..NO MORE ARGUMENTS.. SHE REALLY THOUGHT SHE COULD MAKE ME GET RID OF IT....
ACTUALLY, I WAS SORRY TO SEE HER GO...
I'M GOING TO MISS THE THRILL OF THE CHASE!

THAT WAS VERY BEAUTIFUL, SCHROEDER...WHAT WAS IT?
THAT WAS BEETHOVEN'S SONATA NO. 11, OPUS 22
NOW YOU HAVE ME WORRIED...
LITTLE BY LITTLE BEETHOVEN IS SNEAKING AROUND, OVER, AND UNDER MY MENTAL BLOCK!

I ALWAYS ENJOY READING THE LITTLE NOTES MY MOTHER PUTS IN MY LUNCH..
HMM...SO NOW SHE'S A COMEDIENNE...
WHY? WHAT DOES SHE SAY?
"HELP! I'M BEING HELD PRISONER IN A SCHOOL LUNCH FACTORY!"

IF I WERE A GORILLA LIVING IN THE JUNGLE, I WOULDN'T HAVE TO WALK..
IF I WANTED TO GO SOMEPLACE, I'D LEAP INTO A TREE, AND SWING FROM BRANCH TO BRANCH

HERE'S THE FIERCE GORILLA BEATING HIS CHEST AS THE INHABITANTS OF THE JUNGLE TREMBLE WITH FEAR!
NOW HE SIGHTS THE HELPLESS MAIDEN... HE DECIDES TO CARRY HER OFF...
SHE IS TERRIFIED..
RATS!

MY LIFE HAS BECOME A BORE
EVERYTHING IS THE SAME DAY IN AND DAY OUT...
WHAT I NEED IS A CHANGE

...AND I DON'T CARE IF I NEVER SEE YOU AGAIN! DO YOU HEAR ME?
SHE REALLY HURT YOUR FEELINGS, DIDN'T SHE, CHARLIE BROWN? I HOPE SHE DIDN'T TAKE ALL THE LIFE OUT OF YOU..
NO, NOT COMPLETELY...
BUT YOU CAN NUMBER ME AMONG THE WALKING WOUNDED!

HERE, CHARLIE BROWN...HOLD MY CAT FOR ME WHILE I GO TO THE STORE...
I DON'T KNOW HOW TO HOLD A CAT...I MEAN I'VE... I... HOW DO YOU...I...I... I'VE... I'VE NEVER.....I... I.....I.....
...I.....I.....I.....
OH, GOOD GRIEF!

I'M HOLDING FRIEDA'S CAT FOR HER WHILE SHE GOES TO THE STORE
SAY, I HAVE AN ITCHY NOSE...IF YOU'LL HOLD HIM FOR A SECOND, LINUS, I'LL APPRECIATE IT, AND I'LL...
..WELL, I DON'T KNOW... I'VE NEVER...I MEAN..I..I..
FREE!
OH, NO!!

THAT DIRTY CHARLIE BROWN!
HE TRICKED ME INTO HOLDING FRIEDA'S CAT!
FRIEDA! WHERE ARE YOU? I'VE GOT YOUR CAT! COME, AND GET YOUR CAT!
COME, AND GET YOUR STUPID CAT!!
EXCUSE ME...I WAS MERELY TRYING TO ADD A LITTLE EMPHASIS!

FRIEDA! COME, AND GET YOUR CAT!!
THIS IS TERRIBLE...I CAN'T CARRY THIS CAT AROUND FOR THE REST OF MY LIFE...
THAT DIRTY CHARLIE BROWN! THIS WAS HIS WORK! HE WAS THE ONE WHO TRICKED ME!
AND THE LEAST YOU COULD DO IS LOOK A LITTLE GUILTY!!

Z
Z
MEOW

WELL, WHERE HAVE YOU BEEN? I THOUGHT I WAS GOING TO HAVE TO HOLD THIS CAT FOREVER!
YOU DON'T LIKE CATS!
I DIDN'T SAY THAT!
I JUST DON'T LIKE GETTING STUCK WITH SOME GIRL'S CAT WHILE SHE GOES OFF SOMEPLACE, AND IS GONE ALL DAY!!!
YOU DON'T LIKE GIRLS!

WELL, HI!

BIRDS THINK I'M INTERESTING!

MINE IS THE SORT OF HOME WHERE FRIENDS FEEL THEY CAN JUST DROP IN ANY TIME

IT'S NICE TO HAVE A HOME WHERE YOUR GUESTS FEEL COMFORTABLE
Z
Z

SEE WHAT YOU THINK OF THIS, CHARLIE BROWN..
"DEAR SANTA CLAUS, I AM SOMEWHAT FEARFUL ABOUT WRITING TO YOU THIS YEAR...
I HAVE SO MANY FAULTS IT SEEMS IMPROBABLE THAT YOU WILL WANT TO BRING ME ANY PRESENTS..."
IT'S THE OL' HUMBLE BIT!

I LOVE WINTER!
I ESPECIALLY LOVE THE BEAUTIFUL SNOWFLAKES..
"THEY FLOAT DOWN GENTLY FROM THE SKY, COVERING FOREST AND HILL...
STILL, THERE'S A LOT TO BE SAID FOR SUMMER!

THE BLANKET I CAN SEE....BUT THE THUMB, NO!
THAT CONSTANT SLURPING SIMPLY NAUSEATES ME!
I DON'T THINK I'M GOING TO BE ABLE TO STAND IT....
THERE MUST BE HUNDREDS OF TRAVEL AGENTS WHO WOULD BE ONLY TOO GLAD TO GUIDE YOU TO THE OTHER SIDE OF THE WORLD!

LOOK AT THOSE STUPID BUGS...
THEY DON'T HAVE THE SLIGHTEST IDEA AS TO WHAT IS GOING ON IN THIS WORLD!
WHAT IS GOING ON IN THIS WORLD?
I DON'T HAVE THE SLIGHTEST IDEA!

MOM SAYS COME ON IN FOR SUPPER..
PUNT
???
THE "MAD PUNTER" STRIKES AGAIN!

YOU SAY YOU LEFT YOUR FOOTBALL IN THE BACKYARD LAST NIGHT?
UH HUH... AND THEN, ABOUT TEN O'CLOCK, I WOKE UP, AND I COULD HEAR SOMEONE PUNTING IT ALL OVER THE YARD
BUT WHO IN THE WORLD WOULD BE PUNTING A FOOTBALL AROUND AT TEN O'CLOCK AT NIGHT?
I CAN'T IMAGINE!

PUNT
HAVE YOU SEEN MY FOOTBALL, CHARLIE BROWN? IT SEEMS TO HAVE DISAPPEARED
YOURS, TOO?
THE "MAD PUNTER" HAS STRUCK AGAIN!
IS THERE NO STOPPING THIS FIEND? WILL HE NEVER BE CAUGHT?

IT'S EERIE, THAT'S WHAT IT IS!
IT'S EERIE KNOWING THAT SOMEWHERE OUT IN THAT DARKNESS THE "MAD PUNTER" IS LURKING...
ANYONE WHO OWNS A FOOTBALL WILL NOT SLEEP WELL TONIGHT!

SEE? SOMEONE'S BEEN KICKING A FOOTBALL HERE..
YOU CAN SEE HIS TRACKS IN THE NEW-FALLEN SNOW... HE'S BEEN KICKING IT ALL OVER THE YARD... BACK AND FORTH!
AND THEN HE LEFT! AND HE HEADED IN THIS DIRECTION! IF WE FOLLOW THESE TRACKS, WE RUN RIGHT INTO THE...
..."MAD PUNTER"

YOU CAUGHT THE "MAD PUNTER"?
YUP, WE TRACKED HIM DOWN IN THE NEW-FALLEN SNOW...
WHAT DID YOU DO TO HIM?
NOTHING!
NOTHING?
IT'S ONLY RIGHT TO SHOW COMPASSION ON CHRISTMAS EVE!

AND NOW, AFTER LISTENING TO THE NINTH SYMPHONY, WE'RE READY TO SERVE THE CAKE
WOW!
HAPPY BIRTHDAY, BEETHOVEN!
THIS IS A SIMPLE CEREMONY, BUT VERY MEANINGFUL...
I'LL SAY IT IS...YOU'RE GOING TO HAVE TO CUT THE CAKE..MY EYES ARE TOO FULL OF TEARS!

CAN'T THAT CAT OF YOURS WALK?
OF COURSE, HE CAN WALK, BUT CATS ARE VERY DELICATE CREATURES...THEY DON'T LIKE TO GET THEIR FEET DIRTY!
SANDBAGGER!!

OH OH! HERE COMES "PIG-PEN"
SOMEDAY SOMEBODY'S GOING TO PUT FOUR BOARDS AROUND THAT KID AND HAVE AN "INSTANT SANDBOX"!

DO YOU EVER WORRY ABOUT GROWING UP, CHARLIE BROWN?
ALL THE TIME, FRIEDA..
I DO, TOO... I WORRY ABOUT MY BEING ABLE TO FIT INTO THE RESPONSIBILITIES OF ADULT LIFE AND WOMANHOOD...
OF COURSE, I **DO** HAVE ONE BIG ADVANTAGE...
WHAT'S THAT?
I HAVE NATURALLY CURLY HAIR!
OH, GOOD GRIEF!

I NEED YOUR HELP, CHARLIE BROWN!
FARON'S UP IN A TREE, AND HE CAN'T GET DOWN...
HA! THIS IS WHAT YOU GET FOR HAVING A CAT! YOU'D NEVER CATCH SNOOPY CLIMBING A TREE!
WHAM

WELL, IT TOOK ME SIX WEEKS, BUT I FINALLY FIGURED IT OUT...

ALL IN ALL, HE GAVE HER TWENTY-TWO TURTLE DOVES, THIRTY FRENCH HENS, THIRTY-SIX CALLING BIRDS, FORTY GOLD RINGS, FORTY-TWO GEESE-A-LAYING....

FORTY-TWO SWANS-A-SWIMMING, FORTY MAIDS-A-MILKING, THIRTY-SIX PIPERS PIPING, THIRTY LADIES DANCING, TWENTY-TWO LORDS A-LEAPING, TWELVE FIDDLERS FIDDLING, AND TWELVE PARTRIDGES IN PEAR TREES!

WHEN I GROW UP, I'M GOING INTO RESEARCH
YOU SHOULD BE VERY GOOD AT IT!

WHAT'S THE CURE FOR DISILLUSIONMENT, CHARLIE BROWN?
A CHOCOLATE-CREAM AND A FRIENDLY PAT ON THE BACK
GOOD OL' CHARLIE BROWN!

SNIF?
SNIF?
GULP!
HAPPINESS IS A PIECE OF FUDGE CAUGHT ON THE FIRST BOUNCE!